<u>The Evolution of Computing</u>

The evolution of computing has been marked by remarkable transformations, starting from the earliest mechanical calculators to today's powerful, interconnected digital networks. This journey reflects humanity's relentless quest to enhance computational efficiency and accessibility. Initially, computing was a highly specialized activity, conducted by experts who manually manipulated physical devices to perform calculations. The advent of electronic computers in the mid-20th century, with the development of the ENIAC and UNIVAC, marked the beginning of the digital era. These colossal machines, occupying entire rooms, laid the groundwork for the rapid advancements that followed. The transition from vacuum tubes to transistors and, eventually, to integrated circuits revolutionized the industry, making computers smaller, faster, and more reliable. Each technological leap brought computers closer to mainstream use, setting the stage for the personal computing revolution of the 1980s and beyond.

From Command Line Interfaces (CLI) to Graphical User Interfaces (GUI):

The shift from Command Line Interfaces (CLI) to Graphical User Interfaces (GUI) represents one of the most significant advancements in the history of computing. In the early days, CLI was the norm, requiring users to input text commands to interact with the computer. This mode of operation demanded a high level of expertise, as users needed to memorize complex commands and syntax. The CLI, while powerful, was intimidating to novices and posed a barrier to wider adoption of computing technology. The introduction of GUI in the 1980s, pioneered by systems like the Apple Macintosh and later popularized by Microsoft Windows, transformed this landscape. GUI allowed users to interact with their computers through intuitive visual elements such as icons, windows, and menus. This innovation made computing accessible to a broader audience, enabling even those without technical knowledge to use computers effectively. The GUI's impact is akin to providing drivers with a dashboard full of easily recognizable symbols and controls, instead of requiring them to manually understand and manipulate the engine's inner workings.

The Emergence of Bots and Their Limitations:

As computing continued to evolve, the emergence of bots marked another milestone. Bots, or automated software applications, were designed to perform repetitive tasks with speed and accuracy, ranging from web crawling to customer service interactions. Early bots were relatively simple, capable of executing predefined commands and routines without understanding the context or nuances of human language. For instance, a chatbot might assist customers by answering basic queries or guiding them through a purchase process. However, these bots were limited in their capacity to handle complex or ambiguous requests, often leading to frustration when they failed to comprehend or appropriately respond to user inputs. The limitations of early bots can be likened to having a very efficient but narrowly focused assistant who excels at following specific instructions but struggles when faced with unexpected or nuanced tasks.

Introduction to Intelligent Agents:

The concept of intelligent agents represents a significant leap forward from traditional bots. Intelligent agents are sophisticated systems designed to act autonomously and make decisions based on their environment and interactions. Unlike bots, which follow strict, predefined rules, intelligent agents can learn and adapt, using techniques from artificial intelligence (AI) such as machine learning and natural language processing. These agents are capable of understanding context, recognizing patterns, and improving their performance over time. For example, an intelligent personal assistant like Apple's Siri or Amazon's Alexa can interpret user commands, learn preferences, and provide personalized recommendations. This adaptability and learning capability distinguish intelligent agents from their simpler predecessors, making them far more versatile and effective in a wide range of applications.

Definition and Differentiation from Bots:

Intelligent agents are defined by their ability to operate autonomously, perceive their environment, make decisions, and learn from their experiences. While bots are typically designed for specific, rule-based tasks, intelligent agents can perform complex, multi-step operations that require contextual understanding and adaptability. This distinction is crucial in understanding the potential and limitations of each technology. For instance, a bot may be programmed to scan and index web pages for a search engine, but it lacks the ability to adapt to changes in web content or user behavior without human intervention. In contrast, an intelligent agent can dynamically adjust its strategies based on real-time data, improving its effectiveness over time. This difference is akin to comparing a basic calculator, which performs fixed arithmetic functions, to a human accountant who can analyze financial trends, make projections, and provide strategic advice.

Significance of Bill Gates' Prediction:

The significance of Bill Gates' prediction about the rise of intelligent agents underscores the transformative potential of this technology. Gates envisioned a future where intelligent agents would become integral to our daily lives, enhancing productivity and simplifying complex tasks. His foresight highlighted the shift from static, rule-based systems to dynamic, adaptive ones that can understand and respond to human needs. This prediction is increasingly becoming a reality as intelligent agents permeate various sectors, from healthcare and finance to entertainment and education. The widespread adoption of these agents signifies a paradigm shift in human-computer interaction, where technology not only assists but also anticipates and fulfills user needs. Gates' vision can be compared to the early predictions about the internet's impact; initially met with skepticism, it eventually revolutionized how we communicate, work, and live, reshaping the world in profound and unexpected ways.

The Historical Context

The story of computing is one of rapid innovation and transformative change, marked by the relentless pursuit of more powerful, efficient, and user-friendly technologies. From the mechanical calculating machines of the 19th century to the sophisticated digital systems of today, each era in computing history has brought forth significant advancements that have reshaped industries and everyday life. The historical context of computing reveals a journey that began with basic arithmetic operations and has now evolved into complex, interconnected networks capable of supporting artificial intelligence and autonomous systems. Understanding this historical context provides insight into how far we have come and the foundational principles that continue to drive innovation in the field.

Early Computing and User Interfaces

The Command-Line Era:

In the early days of computing, user interfaces were primarily text-based, relying on command-line interfaces (CLI). This era, which spanned from the 1950s to the early 1980s, required users to interact with computers by typing specific commands into a console or terminal. CLIs were powerful tools, offering direct control over the computer's functions and capabilities. However, they were also highly specialized, demanding a steep learning curve and a deep understanding of the command syntax. For instance, early users of UNIX or MS-DOS needed to memorize a plethora of commands and their parameters to perform even basic tasks. This command-line approach was akin to operating a car by manipulating the engine directly, rather than using a steering wheel and pedals—effective for those with expertise, but inaccessible to the general public.

Introduction of Graphical User Interfaces:

The introduction of graphical user interfaces (GUIs) in the 1980s revolutionized computing by making it accessible to a broader audience.

Pioneered by innovations like the Apple Macintosh and popularized by Microsoft Windows, GUIs replaced complex text commands with intuitive visual elements such as icons, buttons, and menus. This shift transformed the user experience, enabling people to interact with their computers through simple point-and-click actions. GUIs democratized computing, allowing individuals without technical backgrounds to use and benefit from digital technology. This transformation is comparable to the introduction of the automatic transmission in automobiles, which made driving easier and more approachable for everyone, not just skilled mechanics.

Rise of Bots

Chatbots and Their Evolution:

The rise of bots, particularly chatbots, marked a significant milestone in the evolution of human-computer interaction. Early chatbots, such as ELIZA developed in the 1960s, were designed to simulate conversation with users by following scripted responses. These early implementations were fascinating yet limited, as they could only mimic understanding based on predefined patterns and rules. Over time, chatbots evolved, incorporating more advanced technologies like natural language processing (NLP) and machine learning. This evolution enabled them to better understand and respond to human language, making interactions more fluid and meaningful. Modern chatbots, such as those used in customer service and virtual assistants, represent a significant advancement from their early counterparts, offering more sophisticated and context-aware interactions.

Use Cases and Limitations of Early Bots:

Despite their advancements, early bots had significant limitations that hindered their effectiveness in complex scenarios. Initially, bots were employed in various use cases, such as automating repetitive tasks, providing customer support, and assisting in simple information retrieval. For example, a basic chatbot might help users navigate a website or answer frequently asked questions. However, these bots struggled with ambiguity and the nuances of human language, often resulting in frustrating user experiences when faced with unexpected or complex queries. Their limitations were similar to those of a rudimentary machine that could perform a specific function but lacked the adaptability to handle variations or new challenges. These constraints highlighted the need for more intelligent systems capable of learning and evolving from interactions, paving the way for the development of intelligent agents that could better meet user expectations and demands.

The historical context of computing, from the command-line era to the rise of bots, underscores the continuous drive toward more intuitive and powerful technologies. Each stage of this evolution has brought us closer to realizing the full potential of human-computer interaction, with intelligent agents representing the next frontier in this ongoing journey.

Defining Intelligent Agents

Intelligent agents represent a significant advancement in the field of artificial intelligence, combining various technologies to create systems that can perform complex tasks autonomously. Unlike traditional bots, which are typically rule-based and limited in scope, intelligent agents are designed to understand, learn, and adapt to their environments. These capabilities allow them to provide more sophisticated and effective interactions, making them invaluable in numerous applications ranging from customer service to personal assistants.

What Are Intelligent Agents?:

Intelligent agents are autonomous entities that perceive their environment through sensors and act upon that environment using actuators. They are capable of making decisions based on the data they collect, often in real-time, and can learn from their experiences to improve their performance over time. This makes them fundamentally different from traditional bots, which generally operate based on predefined rules and lack the ability to adapt or learn. For example, an intelligent agent in a smart home system might adjust the thermostat based on the residents' preferences and habits, whereas a traditional bot might only follow a set schedule without considering changes in the environment or user behavior.

Characteristics and Capabilities:

Intelligent agents possess several defining characteristics that set them apart from simpler automated systems. First and foremost, they are autonomous, meaning they can operate independently without continuous human intervention. They also exhibit learning capabilities, using machine learning algorithms to improve their performance based on past interactions. Additionally, intelligent agents are designed for contextual understanding, allowing them to interpret and respond to complex, nuanced inputs accurately. This capability is often enhanced by natural language processing (NLP), which enables the agent to understand and generate human language. Finally, intelligent agents can make autonomous decisions, assessing various factors and choosing the best course of action to achieve their goals.

Comparison with Traditional Bots:

The key difference between intelligent agents and traditional bots lies in their ability to adapt and learn. Traditional bots are typically programmed with a fixed set of rules and responses, making them effective for specific, repetitive tasks but limited in their ability to handle unexpected situations or complex queries. For example, a traditional customer service bot might be able to answer common questions about a product but would struggle with nuanced customer concerns that fall outside its programmed knowledge base. In contrast, an intelligent agent can understand the context of a customer's query, learn from previous interactions, and provide more accurate and helpful responses. This adaptability makes intelligent agents far more versatile and capable than traditional bots.

Key Components

Natural Language Processing (NLP):

Natural Language Processing (NLP) is a critical component of intelligent agents, enabling them to understand and generate human language. NLP involves the use of algorithms to process and analyze large amounts of natural language data, allowing the agent to comprehend text or speech inputs and respond in a way that is both relevant and natural. For instance, an intelligent virtual assistant like Amazon's Alexa uses NLP to interpret voice commands and provide appropriate responses, whether it's playing music, setting reminders, or answering questions. The ability to engage in natural, human-like conversations is a cornerstone of what makes intelligent agents so powerful and user-friendly.

Machine Learning (ML):

Machine Learning (ML) is another foundational component of intelligent agents, providing them with the ability to learn from data and improve their performance over time. ML algorithms enable agents to identify patterns, make predictions, and refine their actions based on feedback and new information. For example, a recommendation system in an e-commerce platform uses ML to analyze user behavior and preferences, suggesting products that the user is likely to be interested in. This capability allows intelligent agents to become more accurate and effective the more they are used, continuously enhancing their utility and user experience.

Contextual Understanding:

Contextual understanding is the ability of intelligent agents to grasp the context of interactions, taking into account various factors such as the user's history, the current environment, and the specific situation at hand. This capability allows agents to provide more relevant and personalized responses.

For instance, a context-aware travel assistant can offer tailored suggestions for restaurants and attractions based on the user's location, preferences, and past behavior. Contextual understanding ensures that intelligent agents can deliver more meaningful and useful interactions, improving overall satisfaction and effectiveness.

Autonomous Decision-Making:

Autonomous decision-making is perhaps the most advanced capability of intelligent agents, allowing them to make independent decisions based on their analysis of the environment and objectives. This involves evaluating different options, considering potential outcomes, and selecting the best course of action. Autonomous decision-making is crucial in applications such as autonomous vehicles, where the agent must continuously assess and react to dynamic road conditions, traffic, and other factors to ensure safe and efficient travel. This capability not only enhances the functionality of intelligent agents but also opens up new possibilities for their use in complex, real-world scenarios.

Intelligent agents represent a leap forward in the capabilities of automated systems, combining autonomy, learning, contextual understanding, and decision-making to deliver more sophisticated and effective interactions. By leveraging advanced technologies such as NLP and ML, intelligent agents can perform a wide range of tasks with greater accuracy and adaptability, making them indispensable tools in today's digital landscape.

Technological Foundations

The technological foundations of intelligent agents rest on several key advancements in artificial intelligence (AI) and machine learning (ML), particularly in the areas of natural language processing (NLP) and sophisticated learning algorithms. These technologies enable intelligent agents to perform complex tasks, understand human language, and make informed decisions. By integrating these technologies, developers can create smarter, more responsive agents capable of adapting to various contexts and improving over time.

Natural Language Processing

Techniques and Advancements:

Natural Language Processing (NLP) involves the interaction between computers and humans through natural language. NLP techniques have advanced significantly over the past few decades, driven by the increasing availability of large datasets and the development of more sophisticated algorithms. Early NLP systems relied heavily on rule-based approaches, which required extensive manual programming and were limited in their flexibility and scalability. However, modern NLP techniques leverage statistical methods and deep learning to analyze and generate human language more effectively.

Key advancements in NLP include the development of tokenization, stemming, and lemmatization techniques, which break down text into manageable units and normalize variations in word forms. Named entity recognition (NER) and part-of-speech (POS) tagging are other important techniques that allow systems to identify and categorize elements within a text. Sentiment analysis, machine translation, and text summarization have also seen significant improvements, enabling more nuanced understanding and generation of language.

Major NLP Models

Two of the most influential NLP models in recent years are GPT-4 and BERT:

- GPT-4 (Generative Pre-trained Transformer 4): Developed by OpenAI, GPT-4 is a state-of-the-art language model that can generate coherent and contextually relevant text based on a given prompt. It is trained on a vast corpus of text from the internet, enabling it to produce human-like responses across a wide range of topics. GPT-4's transformer architecture allows it to understand and generate text by capturing long-range dependencies and contextual relationships between words. This model is widely used in applications such as chatbots, content creation, and language translation.

- BERT (Bidirectional Encoder Representations from Transformers): Created by Google, BERT is a groundbreaking model that introduced the concept of bidirectional training, meaning it considers the context from both the left and right sides of a word in a sentence. This approach allows BERT to achieve a deeper understanding of language context and semantics. BERT has been highly successful in various NLP tasks, including question answering, text classification, and named entity recognition, making it a versatile tool for improving the accuracy and performance of NLP applications.

Machine Learning and AI

Supervised vs. Unsupervised Learning:

Machine learning (ML) encompasses various approaches to training algorithms to make predictions or decisions based on data. Two primary types of learning in ML are supervised and unsupervised learning:

- Supervised Learning: In supervised learning, the algorithm is trained on a labeled dataset, meaning that each training example is paired with an output label. The goal is to learn a mapping from inputs to outputs that can be used to make predictions on new, unseen data. Common applications of supervised learning include image classification, spam detection, and medical diagnosis. For example, a supervised learning model might be trained to recognize handwritten digits by learning from a large dataset of labeled digit images.

- Unsupervised Learning: Unsupervised learning, on the other hand, involves training an algorithm on data without labeled outputs. The goal is to identify patterns or structures within the data. Clustering and dimensionality reduction are common unsupervised learning techniques. For instance, an unsupervised learning algorithm might analyze customer purchase data to identify distinct customer segments with similar buying behaviors, even without predefined labels.

Reinforcement Learning:

Reinforcement learning (RL) is a type of machine learning where an agent learns to make decisions by interacting with an environment and receiving feedback in the form of rewards or penalties. The agent's objective is to maximize cumulative rewards over time by learning an optimal policy for action selection. RL has been successfully applied in various domains, including game playing, robotics, and autonomous driving.

A classic example of RL is training an AI to play chess. The agent learns by playing numerous games, adjusting its strategy based on the outcomes and rewards received. Through this process, it develops the ability to make increasingly sophisticated and effective moves, ultimately achieving a high level of proficiency.

Integration of AI Technologies

Combining NLP and ML for Smarter Agents:

The integration of NLP and ML technologies is essential for creating intelligent agents that can understand and interact with humans more effectively. By combining the language understanding capabilities of NLP with the predictive power of ML, developers can build agents that are both responsive and adaptive.

For instance, a customer service chatbot that leverages both NLP and ML can understand the nuances of customer queries and provide accurate, contextually relevant responses.

NLP techniques enable the bot to interpret the language and intent of the user's message, while ML algorithms analyze historical data to predict the best response. Additionally, reinforcement learning can be used to further refine the bot's performance, allowing it to learn from interactions and improve over time.

In a more advanced application, an intelligent personal assistant like Google's Assistant or Apple's Siri uses NLP to understand voice commands and ML to personalize responses based on user behavior and preferences. This seamless integration of technologies enables the assistant to provide a more natural and intuitive user experience, demonstrating the potential of combining NLP and ML to create truly intelligent agents.

The technological foundations of intelligent agents are built on significant advancements in NLP and ML. By leveraging these technologies, intelligent agents can perform complex tasks, understand human language, and make autonomous decisions, driving innovation and transforming how we interact with digital systems.

The Commercialization of Personal Agents

The commercialization of personal agents has revolutionized how individuals interact with technology, offering convenience, efficiency, and personalized experiences. These intelligent systems, capable of understanding and responding to user needs, have become integral to various aspects of daily life. From managing schedules and controlling smart home devices to providing customer service and assisting with online shopping, personal agents are reshaping the consumer technology landscape.

Milestones in the Development of Intelligent Agents

Key Innovations and Breakthroughs:

The journey towards the sophisticated personal agents we have today has been marked by several key innovations and breakthroughs. Early milestones include the development of rule-based systems, which laid the groundwork for more advanced technologies. One of the first significant breakthroughs was the creation of ELIZA in the 1960s, a simple chatbot designed to simulate conversation with users. Despite its limitations, ELIZA demonstrated the potential of automated conversational agents.

The advent of machine learning and natural language processing (NLP) in the 1990s and 2000s brought significant advancements. Techniques such as support vector machines (SVM) and recurrent neural networks (RNN) allowed for more complex pattern recognition and language understanding. The introduction of transformer models, particularly Google's BERT and OpenAI's GPT series, revolutionized NLP by enabling deeper contextual understanding and more human-like text generation.

Another critical milestone was the integration of personal agents into smartphones and smart speakers. Apple's Siri, launched in 2011, was one of the first widely adopted intelligent assistants, followed by Google Now (later Google Assistant) and Amazon Alexa.

These products brought intelligent agents into mainstream use, showcasing their potential to enhance everyday tasks and interactions.

Significant Players in the Industry:

Several major companies have played pivotal roles in the development and commercialization of intelligent agents:

- OpenAI: Known for its cutting-edge research in artificial intelligence, OpenAI has developed some of the most advanced language models, including GPT-3 and GPT-4. These models are used in a variety of applications, from chatbots to content creation tools, setting new standards for what intelligent agents can achieve.

- Google: Google has been a significant player in the AI field, with its contributions to NLP and machine learning through projects like BERT and Google Assistant. Google's ecosystem of AI-powered services, including search, home automation, and mobile applications, exemplifies the integration of intelligent agents into everyday technology.

- Microsoft: Microsoft's Cortana and Azure AI services highlight its commitment to AI and intelligent agents. By integrating AI capabilities into its suite of enterprise and consumer products, Microsoft has enabled businesses and individuals to leverage intelligent agents for productivity and efficiency.

Current Market Landscape

Major Products and Services:

The current market for personal agents is diverse, with a range of products and services tailored to different needs and preferences. Some of the major offerings include:

- Smart Assistants: Devices like Amazon Echo (Alexa), Google Home (Google Assistant), and Apple HomePod (Siri) are popular smart assistants that provide voice-activated control over smart home devices, information retrieval, and personal task management.

- Mobile Assistants: Integrated into smartphones, assistants like Apple's Siri, Google Assistant, and Samsung's Bixby offer hands-free control, navigation, reminders, and more, enhancing the mobile user experience.

- Enterprise Solutions: Companies like Microsoft offer AI-powered tools and services for businesses, such as Azure Cognitive Services, which provide capabilities like language understanding, computer vision, and decision-making support.

- Custom AI Solutions: Platforms like OpenAI's GPT series allow developers to create custom intelligent agents for specific applications, from customer service bots to virtual tutors.

Adoption Rates and Consumer Readiness:

Adoption rates of personal agents have been steadily increasing, driven by their growing capabilities and integration into widely used devices. According to recent surveys, a significant percentage of households in developed countries own at least one smart speaker, with many users relying on them for daily tasks. Mobile assistants are also ubiquitous, with billions of smartphones worldwide equipped with AI-driven features.

Consumer readiness for intelligent agents is high, as people become more accustomed to interacting with AI through various platforms. Factors contributing to this readiness include the convenience of voice-activated controls, the increasing accuracy and utility of AI responses, and the seamless integration of intelligent agents into existing ecosystems. However, challenges remain, such as concerns about privacy and data security, which need to be addressed to ensure widespread trust and acceptance.

The commercialization of personal agents has transformed how we interact with technology, making it more intuitive and accessible. Milestones in AI and NLP have driven significant innovations, with major players like OpenAI, Google, and Microsoft leading the way. The current market offers a diverse range of products and services, with high adoption rates reflecting consumer readiness for these intelligent systems. As technology continues to advance, personal agents will likely become even more integral to our daily lives, further enhancing convenience and efficiency.

Transforming Industries

The integration of intelligent agents is revolutionizing various industries by enhancing efficiency, improving customer experiences, and providing personalized services. From healthcare to finance, education, and customer service, these advanced technologies are driving significant changes and offering innovative solutions to long-standing challenges.

Healthcare

Personalized Health Assistants:

In healthcare, intelligent agents are playing a crucial role in personalizing patient care. Personalized health assistants, powered by AI, can monitor patients' health metrics, provide medication reminders, and offer lifestyle recommendations tailored to individual needs. For example, a diabetic patient can use a health assistant to track blood sugar levels, receive dietary advice, and get reminders to take insulin. These assistants help patients manage chronic conditions more effectively and engage in proactive health management.

Improving Patient Care and Administrative Efficiency:

Intelligent agents are also enhancing patient care by streamlining administrative tasks and improving communication between patients and healthcare providers. AI-driven systems can schedule appointments, manage patient records, and handle billing processes with minimal human intervention. For instance, a virtual assistant can help patients book appointments online, reducing wait times and ensuring better utilization of healthcare resources. Additionally, AI-powered chatbots can answer common patient queries, freeing up medical staff to focus on more complex issues. This integration not only improves patient satisfaction but also boosts the overall efficiency of healthcare facilities.

Finance

Smart Financial Advisors:

In the finance industry, intelligent agents are transforming how individuals manage their finances and make investment decisions. Smart financial advisors use AI to analyze market trends, assess risk profiles, and provide personalized investment recommendations. These advisors can offer tailored advice based on a user's financial goals, risk tolerance, and market conditions. For example, a smart advisor might suggest a diversified investment portfolio for a young professional looking to build wealth over the long term, while recommending more conservative options for a retiree seeking steady income.

Fraud Detection and Risk Management:

Intelligent agents are also crucial in enhancing security and managing risks within the financial sector. AI-driven fraud detection systems can analyze vast amounts of transaction data in real-time, identifying suspicious activities and potential fraud patterns. By using machine learning algorithms, these systems can detect anomalies and flag transactions that deviate from normal behavior, enabling quick response to potential threats. Additionally, intelligent agents assist in risk management by predicting market fluctuations and assessing the impact of various financial decisions, helping institutions mitigate risks and make informed choices.

Education

Personalized Learning Experiences:

The education sector is benefiting from intelligent agents through the creation of personalized learning experiences. AI-powered educational platforms can adapt to individual learning styles and paces, providing customized content and feedback. For instance, a student struggling with math can receive tailored exercises and explanations that target their specific weaknesses, ensuring a more effective learning process. These personalized experiences help students achieve better outcomes and foster a more engaging and supportive educational environment.

Tutoring and Educational Content Generation:

Intelligent agents are also revolutionizing tutoring and educational content generation. Virtual tutors can provide one-on-one assistance to students, answering questions and explaining concepts in real-time. These tutors can simulate a personal classroom experience, offering guidance and support whenever needed. Moreover, AI systems can generate educational content, such as practice questions, study guides, and interactive lessons, tailored to different curriculum standards and student needs. This capability allows educators to provide high-quality, diverse learning materials efficiently, enhancing the overall educational experience.

Customer Service

Enhancing Customer Support:

In customer service, intelligent agents are enhancing support by providing quick and accurate responses to customer inquiries. AI-driven chatbots and virtual assistants can handle a wide range of tasks, from answering frequently asked questions to resolving issues with orders. For example, a chatbot can assist customers in tracking their packages, processing returns, or troubleshooting technical problems. By providing instant support, these agents improve customer satisfaction and reduce the need for human intervention.

Reducing Operational Costs:

Intelligent agents are also helping businesses reduce operational costs by automating routine customer service tasks. By handling a large volume of queries and transactions, AI systems free up human agents to focus on more complex and high-value interactions. This automation reduces the need for extensive customer service teams and lowers overall operational expenses. Additionally, intelligent agents can operate 24/7, ensuring continuous support and improving service availability without the costs associated with staffing around the clock.

Intelligent agents are transforming various industries by introducing advanced, efficient, and personalized solutions. In healthcare, finance, education, and customer service, these technologies are enhancing the quality of services, improving operational efficiency, and providing tailored experiences. As intelligent agents continue to evolve, their impact on these and other industries will only grow, driving further innovation and value creation.

Enhancing Productivity

Intelligent agents are significantly enhancing productivity in both personal and professional settings. By automating routine tasks, managing schedules, and improving decision-making processes, these agents are helping individuals and organizations achieve more with less effort. The integration of personal assistants and advanced AI technologies into daily life and workplaces is driving a new era of efficiency and effectiveness.

Personal Assistants in Daily Life

Scheduling and Task Management:

Personal assistants, such as Apple's Siri, Google Assistant, and Amazon Alexa, have become indispensable tools for managing daily schedules and tasks. These intelligent agents can organize calendars, set appointments, and send reminders, ensuring that users stay on top of their commitments. For example, a busy professional can use a personal assistant to schedule meetings, set deadlines, and even receive alerts about upcoming events, all through simple voice commands. This automation of scheduling and task management reduces the cognitive load on users, allowing them to focus on more important activities and improving overall productivity.

Personal Reminders and Information Retrieval:

In addition to managing schedules, personal assistants excel at providing reminders and retrieving information quickly. They can remind users to take medication, pay bills, or complete specific tasks at designated times. Furthermore, personal assistants can answer questions, provide weather updates, and offer directions, acting as a convenient source of information. For instance, a parent juggling work and family responsibilities can rely on a personal assistant to remind them of school pick-up times, upcoming parent-teacher meetings, and grocery lists. This seamless integration of reminders and information retrieval into daily life helps individuals stay organized and informed, enhancing their ability to manage multiple responsibilities efficiently.

Workplace Efficiency

Automating Routine Tasks:

In the workplace, intelligent agents are transforming how routine tasks are handled, freeing up valuable time for employees to focus on more strategic activities. AI-powered tools can automate a wide range of administrative tasks, such as data entry, invoice processing, and email management. For example, an intelligent agent can automatically sort and categorize incoming emails, flagging important messages for follow-up and archiving less critical ones. This automation reduces the time employees spend on repetitive tasks, increasing their productivity and allowing them to concentrate on higher-value work.

Improving Decision-Making Processes:

Intelligent agents are also enhancing decision-making processes in the workplace by providing data-driven insights and recommendations. These agents can analyze large volumes of data, identify patterns, and generate reports that inform strategic decisions. For instance, a sales team can use an AI-powered analytics tool to identify trends in customer behavior, predict future sales, and optimize their marketing strategies. By providing accurate and timely information, intelligent agents help businesses make informed decisions, improve performance, and stay competitive in their industries.

Case Studies

Real-World Examples of Productivity Enhancements:

Several real-world examples illustrate how intelligent agents are enhancing productivity across various domains:

- Healthcare: In healthcare settings, AI-powered assistants like IBM's Watson for Health are used to analyze medical records, assist in diagnosing diseases, and recommend treatment plans. These intelligent agents help healthcare providers deliver personalized care more efficiently, reducing the time spent on administrative tasks and improving patient outcomes.

- Finance: In the finance industry, intelligent agents such as robo-advisors are helping individuals and businesses manage their investments. For example, Betterment uses AI to provide personalized investment advice, automate portfolio management, and optimize tax strategies. This automation allows clients to achieve their financial goals with minimal manual intervention, enhancing overall productivity.

- Education: In educational institutions, AI-driven platforms like Coursera and Khan Academy are using intelligent agents to provide personalized learning experiences. These platforms adapt to individual learning styles and paces, offering customized content and feedback. As a result, students can learn more effectively and efficiently, achieving better educational outcomes.

- Customer Service: Companies like Zendesk and Salesforce are leveraging AI-powered chatbots to handle customer inquiries and support requests. These chatbots can resolve common issues, answer questions, and escalate complex problems to human agents when necessary. This integration improves customer satisfaction and reduces the workload on customer service teams, enhancing overall operational efficiency.

By automating routine tasks, managing schedules, providing reminders, retrieving information, and improving decision-making processes, these agents are enabling individuals and organizations to operate more efficiently and effectively.

Redefining Human-Technology Interaction

The advent of intelligent agents is fundamentally reshaping how humans interact with technology. These agents are not just tools; they are becoming companions and assistants in our daily lives, requiring a new approach to user experience design, privacy, security, and ethical considerations. As we integrate these advanced systems into more aspects of our lives, it is essential to address the complexities and responsibilities that come with this technological evolution.

User Experience with Intelligent Agents

User Interface Design for Agents:

The user interface (UI) design for intelligent agents is crucial in facilitating seamless and intuitive interactions. Unlike traditional software interfaces that rely heavily on graphical elements, the UI for intelligent agents often emphasizes voice and natural language interactions. This shift demands a focus on clarity, responsiveness, and context-awareness. For instance, a voice-activated assistant like Amazon's Alexa must be able to understand and process natural language commands accurately, providing relevant responses without unnecessary complexity.

Effective UI design for intelligent agents also involves creating interfaces that are accessible and easy to use for people of all ages and technical abilities. This includes ensuring that voice commands are simple and intuitive, visual interfaces are clean and informative, and feedback is immediate and helpful. For example, a smart home assistant should provide visual cues on a screen and audible confirmations to assure users that their commands have been understood and executed. The goal is to create a user experience that feels natural and effortless, enhancing the user's interaction with technology.

Ensuring User Privacy and Security:

As intelligent agents become more integrated into our lives, ensuring user privacy and security is paramount. These systems often have access to sensitive personal information, such as location data, financial details, and private conversations. Protecting this information from unauthorized access and misuse is critical.

Developers must implement robust security measures, including encryption, secure authentication protocols, and regular software updates to protect against vulnerabilities. Additionally, transparent data handling practices are essential to build user trust. Users should be informed about what data is being collected, how it is being used, and who has access to it. For example, privacy settings should be easily accessible, allowing users to control the amount and type of data shared with the intelligent agent. Ensuring user privacy and security not only protects individuals but also fosters a trusted relationship between users and technology.

Ethical Considerations

Bias in AI and Ensuring Fairness:

One of the significant ethical challenges in the development of intelligent agents is addressing bias in AI algorithms. AI systems are trained on vast datasets that may contain inherent biases, leading to unfair or discriminatory outcomes. For instance, an AI-driven hiring tool might favor candidates from certain backgrounds if the training data is not representative of a diverse population.

To ensure fairness, developers must rigorously test and validate AI models against a variety of scenarios and demographics. This involves using diverse and representative datasets, regularly auditing algorithms for bias, and implementing corrective measures when biases are detected. Furthermore, involving ethicists, sociologists, and other stakeholders in the development process can help identify potential biases and develop strategies to mitigate them. Ensuring fairness in AI is not just a technical challenge but a societal imperative to promote equality and prevent discrimination.

Transparency and Accountability:

Transparency and accountability are essential principles in the development and deployment of intelligent agents. Users need to understand how these systems make decisions and what factors influence their outputs. This transparency helps build trust and allows users to make informed choices about using these technologies.

Developers should provide clear documentation and explanations of how intelligent agents work, including the data sources, algorithms, and decision-making processes involved. For example, if an AI system denies a loan application, the user should be able to understand the reasons behind the decision and the criteria used. Additionally, establishing accountability mechanisms, such as audit trails and oversight bodies, ensures that developers and organizations can be held responsible for the actions and decisions of their AI systems. This accountability is crucial for maintaining public trust and ensuring ethical use of technology.

Redefining human-technology interaction through intelligent agents requires a comprehensive approach to user experience, privacy, security, and ethical considerations. By focusing on intuitive UI design, robust privacy protections, and addressing ethical challenges like bias and transparency, we can create intelligent systems that enhance our lives while upholding the values of fairness, trust, and accountability. As we continue to integrate these advanced technologies into our daily routines, it is essential to remain vigilant and proactive in addressing the complexities and responsibilities that come with this new era of human-technology interaction.

Future Prospects and Innovations

The future of intelligent agents is brimming with potential, driven by continuous advancements in artificial intelligence (AI), machine learning (ML), and natural language processing (NLP). These technologies are set to become even more sophisticated, leading to more intuitive, capable, and integrated systems that will reshape various aspects of our lives. As intelligent agents evolve, they will increasingly integrate with emerging technologies, creating new possibilities and transforming society in profound ways.

Predicting Technological Advancements

Upcoming Innovations in AI and ML:

The next decade promises significant breakthroughs in AI and ML, with advancements in areas such as deep learning, reinforcement learning, and neural network architectures. These innovations will enable intelligent agents to perform more complex tasks with greater accuracy and efficiency. For example, improvements in transfer learning will allow AI systems to apply knowledge gained from one domain to another, reducing the need for extensive retraining and making them more adaptable.

Moreover, the development of more advanced algorithms for unsupervised learning will enable intelligent agents to discover patterns and insights from vast amounts of unstructured data without requiring labeled datasets. This capability will enhance their ability to understand and predict human behavior, optimize processes, and provide more personalized experiences.

The Future of Natural Language Understanding:

Natural language understanding (NLU) is set to advance significantly, enabling intelligent agents to comprehend and generate human language with even greater nuance and context. Future NLU models will likely incorporate more sophisticated techniques for understanding context, emotion, and intent, making interactions with intelligent agents more natural and seamless.

For instance, advancements in sentiment analysis will allow agents to detect subtle emotional cues in text and speech, enabling more empathetic and contextually appropriate responses. Additionally, multilingual models will become more proficient, allowing intelligent agents to support a broader range of languages and dialects, facilitating global communication and accessibility.

Integration with Emerging Technologies

Internet of Things (IoT):

The integration of intelligent agents with the Internet of Things (IoT) will create a highly interconnected and responsive environment, where devices and systems work together to provide enhanced experiences and efficiencies. Intelligent agents will serve as the central hubs, coordinating and managing IoT devices in smart homes, cities, and industries.

For example, in a smart home, an intelligent agent could monitor energy usage, optimize heating and cooling systems, manage security cameras, and even reorder household supplies automatically. In industrial settings, these agents could oversee production processes, predict maintenance needs, and optimize supply chains, driving greater efficiency and reducing costs.

Augmented Reality (AR) and Virtual Reality (VR):

The convergence of intelligent agents with augmented reality (AR) and virtual reality (VR) will revolutionize how we interact with digital content and environments. Intelligent agents will enhance AR and VR experiences by providing real-time information, personalized recommendations, and interactive support within immersive environments.

In AR applications, intelligent agents could overlay contextual information on real-world objects, assisting users in tasks such as repairs, navigation, or learning new skills. In VR, they could act as guides, tutors, or collaborators, creating more engaging and interactive experiences in education, gaming, and professional training.

Vision for the Future

The Concept of the "Bond 007" Personal Agent:

Envisioning the future, the concept of a "Bond 007" personal agent represents the pinnacle of intelligent agent capabilities. Such an agent would combine advanced AI, ML, NLU, and integration with IoT, AR, and VR to provide unparalleled support and convenience. This personal agent would be highly adaptive, proactive, and capable of handling a wide range of tasks, from managing personal schedules and finances to ensuring home security and facilitating complex professional activities.

Imagine a personal agent that not only organizes your day but also anticipates your needs, books travel arrangements, provides real-time updates on your investments, assists in professional presentations, and even monitors your health. This agent would act as a seamless extension of yourself, enhancing your capabilities and enabling you to focus on what truly matters.

Potential Societal Impacts and Transformations:

The widespread adoption of advanced intelligent agents will have profound societal impacts, transforming how we live, work, and interact with the world. These agents will democratize access to information and services, bridging gaps in education, healthcare, and economic opportunities. For instance, intelligent agents could provide personalized tutoring to students in remote areas, offer virtual health consultations to underserved populations, and support small businesses with sophisticated tools previously accessible only to large enterprises.

However, these advancements also raise important ethical and societal considerations. Ensuring equitable access to these technologies, addressing privacy and security concerns, and mitigating the risk of job displacement due to automation are critical challenges that must be addressed. As intelligent agents become more integral to our lives, it is essential to foster a balanced and inclusive approach to their development and deployment, ensuring that the benefits are widely shared and potential downsides are thoughtfully managed.

The future prospects and innovations in intelligent agents are vast and transformative. Predicting technological advancements in AI, ML, and NLU, and integrating these agents with emerging technologies like IoT, AR, and VR, will create a more connected, efficient, and personalized world. The vision of a "Bond 007" personal agent exemplifies the potential of these advancements, promising to redefine human-technology interaction and drive significant societal transformations.

Challenges and Barriers to Adoption

The integration and widespread adoption of intelligent agents face several significant challenges and barriers. These range from technical issues related to the accuracy and reliability of AI systems to regulatory and legal concerns surrounding data privacy and intellectual property. Additionally, social and cultural barriers, such as public acceptance and trust in AI, must be addressed to ensure successful adoption. Understanding and overcoming these challenges is crucial for the continued advancement and integration of intelligent agents into various sectors.

Technical Challenges

Improving Accuracy and Reliability:

One of the primary technical challenges in the development of intelligent agents is improving their accuracy and reliability. While AI and machine learning models have made significant strides, they are not infallible. Errors in understanding natural language, misinterpretation of user intent, and incorrect predictions can lead to frustrating user experiences and limit the effectiveness of intelligent agents.

For example, voice-activated assistants may struggle with accents, dialects, or noisy environments, leading to misunderstandings and incorrect responses. Similarly, AI-driven recommendation systems might occasionally suggest irrelevant or inappropriate content, reducing their utility. To address these issues, ongoing research and development efforts focus on enhancing the robustness of AI models, improving their ability to handle diverse inputs, and reducing error rates through more sophisticated algorithms and larger, more representative training datasets.

Handling Complex Tasks and Contexts:

Another significant technical challenge is enabling intelligent agents to handle complex tasks and contexts effectively. Many current systems excel at specific, narrowly defined tasks but struggle when faced with multifaceted problems that require contextual understanding and adaptive decision-making.

For instance, a customer service chatbot might be capable of answering simple queries but fail to resolve more intricate issues that require a deeper understanding of the customer's history and preferences. To overcome this limitation, developers are working on advanced models that can integrate multiple sources of information, reason about context, and dynamically adjust their behavior based on real-time feedback. This involves leveraging techniques such as multi-task learning, context-aware computing, and reinforcement learning to create more versatile and capable intelligent agents.

Regulatory and Legal Issues

Data Privacy and Security Regulations:

Data privacy and security are critical concerns in the deployment of intelligent agents, particularly those that handle sensitive personal information. Regulations such as the

General Data Protection Regulation (GDPR) in Europe and the California Consumer Privacy Act (CCPA) in the United States impose strict requirements on how data is collected, stored, and used. Compliance with these regulations is essential to protect user privacy and avoid legal repercussions.

Intelligent agents must be designed with robust security measures to safeguard data against breaches and unauthorized access. This includes implementing encryption, secure authentication mechanisms, and regular security audits. Additionally, transparency in data practices is vital, ensuring users are informed about what data is being collected, how it is used, and their rights regarding their personal information.

Intellectual Property and Liability Concerns:

Intellectual property (IP) and liability issues also present significant challenges in the adoption of intelligent agents. The creation and use of AI models often involve complex questions about the ownership of generated content and the attribution of responsibility in case of errors or harm caused by AI systems.

For example, if an AI-driven creative tool generates a piece of artwork, determining the ownership rights to that artwork can be legally complex. Similarly, if an autonomous vehicle controlled by an intelligent agent is involved in an accident, attributing liability between the AI developer, the vehicle manufacturer, and the user can be challenging. Addressing these concerns requires the development of clear legal frameworks and guidelines that define IP rights and liability in the context of AI technologies.

Social and Cultural Barriers

Acceptance and Trust in AI:

Public acceptance and trust in AI are crucial for the widespread adoption of intelligent agents. Many people harbor reservations about AI, stemming from fears of job displacement, loss of privacy, and the potential misuse of technology. Building trust requires transparent communication about the benefits and limitations of AI, as well as demonstrable examples of its positive impact on society.

Efforts to increase AI literacy among the general public can help demystify the technology and alleviate fears. For instance, educational initiatives that explain how AI works, its applications, and the safeguards in place to protect users can foster greater understanding and acceptance. Additionally, showcasing successful implementations of intelligent agents that enhance quality of life, such as in healthcare or education, can help build confidence in the technology.

Addressing Fears and Misconceptions:

Addressing fears and misconceptions about AI is essential to overcoming social and cultural barriers. Popular media often portrays AI in dystopian scenarios, contributing to public apprehension. Counteracting these narratives requires a balanced portrayal of AI's potential and the ethical considerations involved in its development.

Developers and policymakers must engage with the public to address concerns and highlight the ethical use of AI. This includes promoting the development and adoption of ethical guidelines for AI, such as fairness, accountability, and transparency principles. By actively addressing fears and misconceptions, stakeholders can build a more informed and receptive environment for the adoption of intelligent agents.

While the adoption of intelligent agents offers significant benefits, it is accompanied by various challenges and barriers. Addressing technical challenges related to accuracy and complexity, navigating regulatory and legal issues, and overcoming social and cultural barriers are all critical steps toward realizing the full potential of intelligent agents. Through concerted efforts in research, regulation, and public engagement, we can create a future where intelligent agents enhance productivity, improve quality of life, and operate within ethical and legal frameworks that ensure their responsible use.

Practical Implementation

Implementing intelligent agents effectively requires a comprehensive approach that spans development, deployment, and continuous improvement. By leveraging the right tools and platforms, adhering to best practices, ensuring seamless integration and scalability, and maintaining ongoing updates and improvements, developers can create robust and responsive intelligent agents.

Developing Intelligent Agents

Tools and Platforms for Building Agents:

Developing intelligent agents necessitates utilizing a range of tools and platforms designed to facilitate AI and machine learning development. Some of the most popular and powerful tools include:

- TensorFlow and PyTorch: These open-source machine learning frameworks provide comprehensive libraries for building and training AI models. They offer flexibility and scalability, making them suitable for both research and production environments.

- Dialogflow and Microsoft Bot Framework: These platforms are specifically designed for creating conversational agents and chatbots. They offer pre-built integrations with various messaging services and provide natural language understanding (NLU) capabilities to handle user interactions.

- OpenAI GPT-3 and GPT-4 APIs: These APIs allow developers to leverage powerful language models for generating human-like text and understanding context. They can be integrated into applications to provide advanced conversational capabilities and content generation.

- Amazon SageMaker and Google AI Platform: These cloud-based platforms provide end-to-end solutions for building, training, and deploying machine learning models. They offer scalability, integrated development environments, and tools for monitoring and managing AI workflows.

Best Practices for Development:

When developing intelligent agents, adhering to best practices ensures that the resulting systems are robust, efficient, and user-friendly. Key best practices include:

- Define Clear Objectives: Start with a clear understanding of the problem you are trying to solve and the specific goals of the intelligent agent. This helps guide the development process and ensures that the agent meets user needs effectively.

- Use High-Quality Data: The quality of the training data directly impacts the performance of the intelligent agent. Use diverse, representative, and high-quality datasets to train models and regularly update the data to reflect changing trends and behaviors.

- Iterative Development: Adopt an iterative development approach, continually testing and refining the agent based on feedback and performance metrics. This helps identify and address issues early in the development cycle.

- Focus on User Experience: Design the user interface and interactions with the end-user in mind. Ensure that the agent is intuitive, responsive, and capable of handling a wide range of user inputs gracefully.

- Security and Privacy: Implement robust security measures to protect user data and ensure compliance with relevant privacy regulations. This includes encryption, secure authentication, and transparent data handling practices.

Deploying and Scaling

Integration with Existing Systems:

Deploying intelligent agents often requires integration with existing systems and infrastructure. This can involve connecting the agent to databases, APIs, and other software applications to ensure seamless operation. Key considerations for integration include:

- Compatibility: Ensure that the intelligent agent is compatible with the existing technology stack and can communicate effectively with other systems. This may involve using middleware or APIs to facilitate integration.

- Data Synchronization: Maintain consistent and accurate data across all integrated systems. Implement data synchronization mechanisms to ensure that information is up-to-date and correctly shared between the intelligent agent and other applications.

- Security: Protect data during integration by using secure communication protocols and access controls. Ensure that only authorized systems and users can interact with the intelligent agent.

Ensuring Scalability and Performance:

Scalability and performance are critical factors in the successful deployment of intelligent agents. As user demand grows, the system must be able to handle increased load without compromising performance. Strategies for ensuring scalability and performance include:

- Cloud Infrastructure: Utilize cloud platforms such as AWS, Google Cloud, or Microsoft Azure to leverage scalable infrastructure and services. These platforms provide auto-scaling, load balancing, and distributed computing capabilities to manage varying workloads.

- Performance Optimization: Optimize the performance of AI models and algorithms by fine-tuning hyperparameters, reducing model complexity, and using efficient data processing techniques. Regularly monitor and profile the system to identify and address performance bottlenecks.

- Load Testing: Conduct load testing to simulate high-traffic scenarios and evaluate the system's performance under stress. This helps identify potential issues and ensures that the intelligent agent can handle peak loads effectively.

Maintaining and Improving Agents

Continuous Learning and Updates:

Maintaining intelligent agents involves continuous learning and updates to keep them relevant and effective. This requires ongoing monitoring, retraining, and fine-tuning of AI models based on new data and user interactions. Key practices for continuous learning and updates include:

- Regular Retraining: Periodically retrain AI models using fresh data to capture evolving trends and behaviors. This helps maintain the accuracy and relevance of the intelligent agent's responses.

- Automated Updates: Implement automated update mechanisms to deploy new models and improvements seamlessly. This ensures that the agent remains up-to-date without requiring manual intervention.

- Performance Monitoring: Continuously monitor the performance of the intelligent agent using metrics such as response accuracy, latency, and user satisfaction. Use these insights to guide further improvements and optimizations.

User Feedback and Iterative Improvements:

User feedback is invaluable for refining and enhancing intelligent agents. By actively soliciting and analyzing feedback, developers can identify areas for improvement and implement changes that enhance the user experience. Key practices for leveraging user feedback include:

- Feedback Mechanisms: Provide users with easy-to-use feedback mechanisms, such as in-app surveys, feedback buttons, or conversational prompts. Encourage users to share their experiences and suggestions for improvement.

- Analyze Feedback: Systematically analyze user feedback to identify common issues, trends, and areas for enhancement. Use this information to prioritize development efforts and address the most impactful concerns.

- Iterative Improvements: Adopt an iterative approach to development, making incremental improvements based on user feedback and performance data. Regularly release updates and enhancements to keep the intelligent agent responsive to user needs.

The practical implementation of intelligent agents involves a holistic approach encompassing development, deployment, and continuous improvement. By leveraging the right tools and platforms, adhering to best practices, ensuring seamless integration and scalability, and maintaining ongoing updates and improvements, developers can create intelligent agents that are robust, responsive, and capable of delivering significant value to users.

Recap of Key Points

The journey from simple bots to sophisticated intelligent agents has been marked by significant advancements in technology, particularly in AI and machine learning. Early bots, with their limited capabilities, have evolved into complex systems capable of understanding and responding to human language, learning from interactions, and making autonomous decisions. This evolution has been driven by breakthroughs in natural language processing (NLP), machine learning (ML), and the integration of AI technologies, resulting in intelligent agents that are more versatile and capable than ever before.

Intelligent agents are transforming various industries by enhancing efficiency, improving customer experiences, and providing personalized services. In healthcare, they offer personalized health assistants and streamline administrative tasks. In finance, they provide smart financial advisors and enhance fraud detection. In education, they create personalized learning experiences and generate educational content. In customer service, they enhance support and reduce operational costs. These agents are also redefining human-technology interaction by improving user interfaces, ensuring privacy and security, and addressing ethical considerations such as bias and transparency.

The Transformative Potential of Intelligent Agents:

The potential of intelligent agents to transform our lives is immense. By automating routine tasks, managing schedules, and providing personalized recommendations, these agents enhance productivity both in personal and professional settings. They integrate seamlessly with emerging technologies like the Internet of Things (IoT), augmented reality (AR), and virtual reality (VR), creating more connected and responsive environments. Looking ahead, advancements in AI and ML will continue to drive the capabilities of intelligent agents, enabling them to perform even more complex tasks with greater accuracy and efficiency.

Call to Action:

As we stand on the brink of this technological revolution, it is essential to embrace and explore the potential of intelligent agents. Whether you are an individual looking to enhance your daily life, a business aiming to improve efficiency, or a developer seeking to innovate, there are numerous opportunities to leverage these advanced systems. By adopting intelligent agents, you can unlock new levels of productivity, creativity, and convenience.

Future Trends to Watch and Personal Takeaways:

Looking forward, several trends will shape the future of intelligent agents. These include further advancements in natural language understanding, the integration of AI with emerging technologies, and the development of more robust and adaptable AI models.

Additionally, ethical considerations such as ensuring fairness, transparency, and accountability will continue to be crucial in the development and deployment of intelligent agents.

Personal takeaways from this journey include the importance of staying informed about technological advancements, being proactive in addressing ethical and security concerns, and continuously seeking to improve and adapt intelligent systems. By doing so, we can harness the full potential of intelligent agents and drive meaningful transformations in our lives and society.

The journey from bots to intelligent agents represents a significant leap in technology, offering transformative potential across various domains. Embrace the opportunities presented by intelligent agents, stay informed about future trends, and be proactive in ensuring ethical and responsible use. The future of intelligent agents is bright, and by exploring their potential, we can create a more efficient, connected, and innovative world.

Glossary of Key Terms

- Artificial Intelligence (AI): The simulation of human intelligence processes by machines, especially computer systems. These processes include learning, reasoning, and self-correction.

- Machine Learning (ML): A subset of AI that involves the use of algorithms and statistical models to enable computers to improve their performance on a task through experience and data.

- Natural Language Processing (NLP): A field of AI focused on the interaction between computers and humans through natural language. It involves enabling computers to understand, interpret, and generate human language.

- Intelligent Agent: An autonomous entity that uses sensors to perceive its environment and actuators to take actions to achieve specific goals. Intelligent agents can learn from their experiences and adapt to new situations.

- Bot: A software application that runs automated tasks over the internet. Simple bots execute repetitive tasks, while more advanced bots can interact with users and provide specific services.

- Command Line Interface (CLI): A user interface that allows users to interact with the computer by typing text commands into a console or terminal.

- Graphical User Interface (GUI): A user interface that allows users to interact with electronic devices using visual elements such as icons, buttons, and menus.

- Deep Learning: A subset of ML involving neural networks with many layers (deep neural networks) that can learn and make intelligent decisions from large amounts of data.

- Reinforcement Learning: An area of ML where an agent learns to make decisions by performing actions in an environment to maximize some notion of cumulative reward.

- Internet of Things (IoT): A network of physical devices, vehicles, appliances, and other items embedded with sensors, software, and connectivity, enabling them to collect and exchange data.

- Augmented Reality (AR): An interactive experience where digital information (images, sounds, etc.) is overlaid on the real world in real time.

- Virtual Reality (VR): A simulated experience that can be similar to or completely different from the real world, typically involving immersive, computer-generated environments.

Recommended Reading and Resources

1. Books:

   - "Artificial Intelligence: A Modern Approach" by Stuart Russell and Peter Norvig

   - "Deep Learning" by Ian Goodfellow, Yoshua Bengio, and Aaron Courville

   - "Hands-On Machine Learning with Scikit-Learn, Keras, and TensorFlow" by Aurélien Géron

2. Online Courses:

   - Coursera: "Machine Learning" by Andrew Ng

   - edX: "Artificial Intelligence" by Columbia University

- Udacity: "Deep Learning Nanodegree"

3. Research Papers:

   - "Attention Is All You Need" by Vaswani et al. (introducing the Transformer model)

   - "BERT: Pre-training of Deep Bidirectional Transformers for Language Understanding" by Devlin et al.

4. Websites and Blogs:

   - OpenAI: https://www.openai.com/

   - Google AI Blog: https://ai.googleblog.com/

   - Towards Data Science: https://towardsdatascience.com/

5. Tools and Platforms:

   - TensorFlow: https://www.tensorflow.org/

   - PyTorch: https://pytorch.org/

   - Dialogflow: https://dialogflow.cloud.google.com/

- Microsoft Bot Framework: https://dev.botframework.com/

www.ingramcontent.com/pod-product-compliance
Lightning Source LLC
Chambersburg PA
CBHW070315230526
45470CB00002B/883